CENGAGE Learning

Novels for Students, Volume 26

Project Editor: Ira Mark Milne

Editorial: Jennifer Greve

Rights Acquisition and Management: Margaret Chamberlain-Gaston, Leitha Etheridge-Sims, Kelly Quin, Tracie Richardson **Manufacturing**: Drew Kalasky

Imaging and Multimedia: Lezlie Light **Product Design**: Pamela A. E. Galbreath, Jennifer Wahi **Vendor Administration**: Civie Green

Product Manager: Meggin Condino

For more information, contact
Gale
27500 Drake Rd.
Farmington Hills, MI 48331-3535

Or you can visit our Internet site at http://www.gale.com **ALL RIGHTS RESERVED**

While every effort has been made to ensure the reliability of the information presented in this publication, Gale does not guarantee the accuracy of the data contained herein. Gale accepts no payment for listing; and inclusion in the publication of any organization, agency, institution, publication, service, or individual does not imply endorsement of the editors or publisher. Errors brought to the attention of the publisher and verified to the satisfaction of the publisher will be corrected in future editions.

ISBN-13: 978-0-7876-8683-3
ISBN-10: 0-7876-8683-2
eISBN-13: 978-1-4144-2933-5
eISBN-10: 1-4144-2933-9
ISSN 1094-3552

Printed in the United States of America
10 9 8 7 6 5 4 3 2 1

Ulysses

James Joyce

1922

Introduction

Ulysses, by James Joyce, is a challenge to understand. It is at once a masterpiece and an anomaly, a novel that stretches the form and content of the genre of which it is a part. At the same time that *Ulysses* uses Homer's *Odyssey* as a major literary referent, the work heralds the end of the nineteenth-century novel as it was commonly understood. It takes readers into the inner realms of human consciousness using the interior monologue style that came to be called stream of consciousness. In addition to this psychological characteristic, it gives a realistic portrait of the life of ordinary people living in Dublin, Ireland, on June 16, 1904. First published in its entirety in France in 1922, the novel was the subject of a famous obscenity trial in 1933, but was found by a U.S. district court in New York to be a work of art. The furor over the novel made Joyce a celebrity. In the long run, the work placed him at the forefront of the modern period of the early 1900s when literary works, primarily in the first two decades, explored interior lives and subjective reality in a new idiom, attempting to probe the human psyche in order to understand the human condition.

Joyce supplied a schema for *Ulysses* that divides and labels the novel's untitled episodes, linking each to the *Odyssey* and identifying other structural and thematic elements. The headings provided in this schema are used in the plot summary below, as is customary in literary analysis of this work. In the novel itself, there are three sections marked with roman numerals but no other explicit headings. The first line of each episode in the novel appears in small capital letters. The schema can be found in a number of works on Joyce; one of these is *Reading Joyce's Ulysses*, by Daniel R. Schwarz. For explanations of references and parallels to Homer's epic, readers will find Don Gifford's exhaustive work, *"Ulysses" Annotated*, indispensable.

Despite Faulkner's roots in the South, he readily condemns many aspects of its history and heritage in *Absalom, Absalom!*. He reveals the unsavory side of southern morals and ethics, including slavery. The novel explores the relationship between modern humanity and the past, examining how past events affect modern decisions and to what extent modern people are responsible for the past.

Author Biography

James Augustine Joyce was born in Dublin, Ireland, on February 2, 1882, the eldest of ten children of John Stanislaus Joyce and Mary Jane Joyce. At age six in 1888, Joyce began his Jesuit education at Clongowes Wood, a boarding school. After that, he attended Belvedere College, a Catholic day school in Dublin. Joyce attended University College in Dublin from 1898 to 1902 and graduated with a degree in modern languages. By this time, he was already writing both poetry and prose sketches. He went to Paris to study medicine for a year but returned to Dublin when his mother was in the final stage of a terminal illness. He taught briefly and published some stories and poems. Then in 1904, he met and began a lifelong relationship with a semi-literate hotel chambermaid, Nora Barnacle, and shortly thereafter, the couple relocated to the town of Pola on the Adriatic Sea where briefly Joyce taught in a local Berlitz school. The following year, Joyce and Barnacle moved to Trieste, where they made their home for the next ten years, except for a brief time in Rome. Married some years later, the couple had two children, Giorgio and Lucia, both born in Trieste.

As early as 1903, Joyce had begun working on an autobiographical work, tentatively titled *Stephen Hero*, and on his collection of short stories, which was ultimately published as *Dubliners* in 1914. He published a collection of poetry, *Chamber Music*, and then revised and expanded *Stephen Hero* and published it as *Portrait of the Artist as a Young Man*, which was serialized in the magazine *Egoist* in 1914 and 1915. In 1915, Joyce and his wife moved to Zurich, where he worked on *Ulysses*, allowing excerpts from the novel to appear in *Egoist* and a New York magazine, *Little Review*. In 1919, he and his wife returned to Trieste and shortly thereafter settled in Paris.

In 1920, *Little Review* stopped serial publication of *Ulysses*, which was drawing obscenity charges in the United States. It was clear to Joyce that the completed novel could not find a U.S. or British publisher. As it happened, an American expatriate in Paris, Sylvia Beach, published the work with the imprint of her bookshop, Shakespeare and Company. The book appeared, as Joyce requested, on his birthday, February 2, 1922. Seen as scandalous and worthy of suppression, the book created a furor and made Joyce a literary celebrity.

During the 1920s, Joyce underwent a series of eye operations. The next decade was also darkened by the apparent mental decline of his daughter, Lucia, who was committed to an asylum in 1936. Joyce completed *Finnegans Wake* in 1938, which was published the following year to generally hostile reviews. He lived briefly in the French village St. Gérand-le-Puy near Vichy and then moved back to Zurich. He died there on January 13, 1941, after surgery for a perforated ulcer. Nora Joyce lived on in Zurich until her death in 1951.

Foreword, District Court Decision, and Letter from Joyce

The 1934 edition of *Ulysses* begins with a Foreword written by Morris L. Ernst, a Random House defense attorney involved in the obscenity case against the novel. Ernst applauds the decision of John M. Woolsey, the presiding judge, to rule against the charge of obscenity and allow the novel to be published in the United States. Ernst claims this judicial decision marks a "New Deal in the law of letters." The attorney explains the complications involved in the definition and application of obscenity and links this release from "the legal compulsion for squeamishness in literature" with the repeal of Prohibition, which occurred also in the first week of December 1933.

Next, Judge Woolsey describes in his opinion Joyce's accomplishment:

> [He] attempted … with astonishing success—to show how the screen of consciousness with its ever-shifting kaleidoscopic impressions carries … not only what is in the focus of each man's observation of the actual things about him, but also in a penumbral zone residua of past

impressions, some recent and some drawn up by association from the domain of the subconscious.

This technique, Judge Woolsey explains, is like "a multiple exposure on a cinema film." In essence, the judge concludes, Joyce's effort was to show how the minds of his characters operate. Woolsey also expounds on the legal meaning of the term, obscenity, as a characteristic in a work intended "to stir the sex impulses or to lead to sexually impure and lustful thoughts." Read in its entirety, he maintains, the novel does not have this effect. Rather, it serves as "a somewhat tragic and very powerful commentary on the inner lives of men and women."

Also included is the April 2, 1933, letter of James Joyce to Bennett A. Cerf, the Random House publisher who decided to print *Ulysses*. Joyce explains the assistance he received from Ezra Pound and from Sylvia Beach, owner of an English bookstore in Paris which first published the novel. He also explains some of the difficulties in the United Kingdom and in the United States regarding the subsequent distribution and sale of this first edition.

Media Adaptations

- An audio book abridgement of *Ulysses*, read by Jim Norton and Marcella Riordan, became available in 1995 from Naxos. The four cassettes are in total five hours long.

- In 1967, Joseph Strick directed *Ulysses*, starring Milo O'Shea in the role of Leopold Bloom. As of 2007, this film was available on DVD.

- In 2006, Odyssey Pictures released *Bloom: All of Life in One Extraordinary Day*, directed by Sean Walsh and starring Stephen Rea as Leopold Bloom.

I: Telemachia

TELEMACHUS

Early on June 16, 1904, Stephen Dedalus, the Englishman Haines, and Malachi Mulligan, called Buck, have breakfast at the Martello Tower at Sandycove on Dublin Bay which Stephen rents. Irreverently, Buck shaves as though he is celebrating mass and says a mock grace before the three eat breakfast. Buck also alludes to Stephen's "absurd" Greek name. Stephen feels imposed upon by the Oxford student Haines, who was invited by Buck but has been disruptive during the previous night with a bad dream. Though it is Stephen's place, Buck seems to have taken charge, serving the food, taking possession of the key to the tower, and getting money from Stephen for drinks later in the day. Stephen is preoccupied with thoughts of his recently deceased mother, having dreamed of her the night before. Buck goes off for a swim, Haines and Stephen smoke a cigarette, and both Haines and Buck refer briefly to Stephen's theory about *Hamlet*. Haines draws a parallel between the Martello Tower and Hamlet's castle and then asks Stephen about his belief in a personal God. Stephen responds that he is "the servant of two masters … an English and an Italian," meaning "the imperial British state" and "the holy Roman catholic and apostolic church." He adds there is a third master, Ireland, "who wants [him] for odd jobs." It is about 8:00 a.m. when Stephen heads off to the boys' boarding school where he teaches. Buck asks that they meet at 12:30 at the pub called the Ship. As Stephen leaves, he promises himself not to sleep at the tower the coming night since Buck has taken it over. Stephen calls him a "usurper." This allusion to the usurper King Claudius in *Hamlet*, as well as several references to Hamlet and to Stephen's brooding depression, all suggest parallels between Stephen and the melancholy prince.

NESTOR

It is 10 a.m., and Stephen is teaching an ancient Greek history class in a boys' school in Dalkey, drilling the students on Pyrrhus and picking on an unprepared student named Armstrong. It is a half-day at school, and the boys are eager to go out on the field and play soccer. Next, Stephen asks the students to read from John Milton's "Lycidas," an elegy on the death by drowning of Milton's friend. Stephen then challenges the students to solve a paradoxical riddle. The class ends, and the students leave in haste, except for one, Cyril Sargent, who remains behind to get help with his math problems. Bending over Cyril, Stephen thinks about how some woman gave birth to this boy and loves him, thoughts associated in Stephen's mind with the recent death of his own mother. Cyril leaves, and Stephen goes to collect his pay from the headmaster, Garrett Deasy, who expresses misogynistic and anti-Semitic views and wants a letter he has written on hoof-and-mouth disease to be published in local newspapers. He gives a copy of the letter to Stephen, asking him to take it to news offices where he has contacts. Mr. Deasy suggests that Stephen will not long work as a teacher. Agreeing that he is more learner than teacher, Stephen leaves with Mr. Deasy's letter, laughing at the headmaster's opinions and reminding himself that he has a date to meet Buck at the Ship pub at 12:30.

PROTEUS

Including very little dialogue, the third episode, which begins at 11 a.m., is the most interior of the first three. In this section, Stephen walks along Sandymount Strand, spending an hour and a half on the beach, thinking about the difference between the objective world and how it appears to his eyes. He spies two midwives, one with a bag in which Stephen imagines there is a miscarried fetus. He considers the possibility of an umbilicus long enough to serve as a telephone line across which one could phone up navel-free Eve in Eden. He thinks about the conception of Jesus and how, according to the Nicene Creed, Jesus was said to be of the essence of God, not created out of nothing as man was. The wind reminds him that he has to go to the newspaper offices with Mr. Deasy's letter. Briefly he considers visiting his aunt, but then he misses her street. He thinks about being ashamed of his family when he was little. Headed toward the Pigeon House, he thinks of Mary and how her pregnancy was attributed to a bird. He thinks back to Paris and remembers a conversation with Kevin Egan on nationalism. At the edge of the water, he looks back, searching the view for the Martello Tower and again promising himself not to sleep there this night. He sees a dog running toward him followed by a couple who are intent on picking cockles. He thinks about his dream the night before, in which a man with a melon took him along a red carpet. When the couple passes Stephen, he thinks of a poem and writes it down on a scrap of paper torn from Deasy's letter. When he decides to leave the beach, he urinates, picks his nose, and then looks around to see if anyone is observing him.

II: Odyssey

CALYPSO

The fourth episode occurs at the same time as episode one. It is 8 a.m. at 7 Eccles Street, and Leopold Bloom is in the kitchen getting milk for the cat and a breakfast tray ready for his wife, Marion, called Molly, who is still in bed. Leopold loves organ meat and fancies a fried kidney for his breakfast, so he goes around the corner to a butcher to buy one. Back in the house, he fixes toast for Molly, boils water, and sets the kidney to fry in butter. Upstairs, he brings Molly her breakfast and gives her a card and letter. The letter is from Hugh Boylan, called Blazes, and Leopold sees her hide it under the pillow. She asks him what the word, metempsychosis, means. He has received a letter from their daughter, Millie, which he takes downstairs and reads while he eats. Bloom is wearing his good black suit because at 11 a.m. today he is attending the funeral of his friend Patrick Dignam. After breakfast, he goes to the outhouse to defecate. The church bells toll the hour.

LOTUSEATERS

Leopold Bloom heads in a roundabout way to a post office where he picks up a letter from Martha Clifford, with whom he is conducting a clandestine, erotic correspondence using the pseudonym Henry Flower. With the letter in his pocket, he runs into an acquaintance, C. P. McCoy, who talks to Bloom about Dignam's death and asks that Bloom enter his name as an attendant though he will not be at the funeral. Off by himself, Leopold reads Martha's letter and wonders what kind of woman she really is. Like its parallel episode in the *Odyssey*, this episode is full of indolence and repeated references to smoking and opiates, which Leopold associates with the East and with Molly, who is from Gibraltar. He enters All Hallows, the incense-filled Catholic Church, and observes part of the mass. At 10:15 a.m., he heads to the chemist to buy some face cream for Molly. There he thinks of chloroform and laudanum. The cream must be prepared. The chemist asks for the empty bottle, which Leopold has neglected to bring. Leopold buys a bar of soap and plans to return for the cream. Outside, he meets Bantam Lyons, who wants a newspaper so he can check on the Gold Cup horserace scheduled to run this day. Bloom offers his paper, saying he was going to throw it away, and Lyons rushes off to place a bet, misconstruing Bloom's comment for a tip on the long-shot racehorse named Throwaway. Bloom resolves to have a bath, envisioning himself lying back in the water, his penis floating like a flower.

HADES

In a funeral procession from Sandymount to Prospect Cemetery in Glasnevin, north of Dublin, at 11 a.m., Bloom travels in a carriage with Jack Power, Martin Cunningham, and Simon Dedalus. As they leave the village, shop blinds are drawn down and people on the street tip their hats in respect. Bloom notices Stephen walking along and mentions it to his father, Simon Dedalus. Bloom thinks of his own son, Rudy, who died just a few days after birth and would be eleven years old now had he lived. They pass Blazes Boylan and the other men call to him, which secretly embarrasses Bloom, who knows Boylan will visit Molly at 4 p.m. Mr. Power asks about the concert tour, referring somewhat disrespectfully to Molly as "*Madame*." It is 11:20 a.m., and Bloom thinks of Mrs. Fleming coming into 7 Eccles Street to clean. They pass Reuben J. Dodd, the Jewish moneylender, from whom each of them, except for Bloom, has borrowed money. They comment about how Dodd's son almost drowned in the Liffey, and when a boatman saved him, the father gave him a small bit of money as thanks. Power comments that suicide is the worst death, a family disgrace; Cunningham cuts him off, saying, "We must take a charitable view of it." Bloom sees this as a kindness from Cunningham who knows that Bloom's father was a suicide. At the cemetery, Simon Dedalus cries at the grave of his recently deceased wife, May. A service is given in the chapel and some brief words spoken at the grave. As the mourners disperse, a reporter, Joe Hynes, asks Bloom for his full name and if he can identify a thirteenth man at the gravesite. Bloom cannot name the man in the mackintosh, but he does remember to ask that McCoy's name be added to the list of those present.

AEOLUS

This episode takes place in the *Freeman* newspaper offices. The text here is divided by headlines like those appearing in a newspaper. Bloom gets a copy of the advertisement for Keyes tea and then heads into the *Telegraph* printing room and speaks to the foreman, City Councillor Nanetti, who is in conversation with Hynes about his report on Dignam's funeral. Nanetti wants Bloom to get Keyes to agree to advertise his tea in the paper for three months. Bloom suspects Keyes wants the ad to run only for two months. Bloom goes into the *Telegraph* office, where Simon Dedalus and others are listening to Ned Lambert, who is making fun of a patriotic speech by Dan Dawson. J. J. O'Molloy enters, knocking into Bloom with the doorknob. Stephen Dedalus comes in and hands Deasy's letter to Crawford, who decides to publish it. A group, including Stephen, heads out to a pub, pushing past Bloom as they leave. Bloom wants Crawford to agree to run the Keyes ad for two months rather than three, but Crawford rejects the idea.

LESTRYGONIANS

Bloom goes past a candy store and someone hands him a throw-away announcement of the arrival of an American evangelist. He passes Dilly Dedalus and feels sorry for the motherless child and condemns the Catholic Church for forcing people to have more children than they can afford. He thinks of the term, parallax, recalling his morning discussion with Molly about metempsychosis. Sandwich board men weave their way through the pedestrians, advertising Hely's, one letter on each board. Bloom meets Jossie Breen on the street, his girlfriend from years before, and they talk about Mina Purefoy, who is in protracted labor at the maternity hospital. Repeatedly his thoughts go back to Rudy's neonatal death, to the pain of labor, to the fact that stillborns "are not even registered." As a cloud blots the sun, Bloom thinks about the seasons of life, of Dignam's funeral, and Mrs. Purefoy giving birth. It all seems meaningless to him. Near an optometrist's office, he thinks again about parallax and holds up his little finger to cover the sun; doing so makes him recall an evening walk with Molly and Blazes Boylan, and now Bloom wonders if the two of them were touching then or holding hands. Bloom tosses the announcement into the Liffey.

Eager for his lunch, Bloom leaves one restaurant where the customers are eating rudely and enters Davy Byrne's for a cheese sandwich and glass of burgundy wine. There Nosey Flynn asks about Molly's tour and in mentioning Boylan reminds Bloom of the upcoming meeting between his wife and Blazes. Flynn discusses the upcoming Gold Cup. Two flies stuck together on a window remind Bloom of a time when Molly fed him seedcake out of her mouth and they had sex. There is a big difference between their relationship then and as it is now; he thinks, "Me. And me now."

Elsewhere in the restaurant, men gossip about Bloom, about his work, his involvement with the Freemasons, his refusal to sign his name to contracts. As Bloom leaves, Bantam Lyons comes in, whispering about Bloom's tip on the horse Throwaway. Outside, Bloom walks along calculating what he may make if he sells certain ads for the newspaper. Then he spots Boylan on the street and ducks into the National Museum to avoid him.

SCYLLA AND CHARYBDIS

At the National Library, Stephen Dedalus puts forth some of his literary and philosophical views, along with his biographical reading of *Hamlet*, to a circle of men in the director's office. The group includes the Quaker librarian Thomas W. Lyster, the literary critic and essayist John Eglinton, and the poet, A. E. To these men, Stephen suggests that Shakespeare identified with King Hamlet, that he saw in Prince Hamlet a version of his own son Hamnet who died as a child, and that Queen Gertrude is a dramatic version of Shakespeare's own wife, Ann Hathaway. A. E. objects to a biographical reading of the play, asserting that the text of the play ought to be the focus of any interpretation of it. The librarian Mr. Best comes into the office. Best has been showing Haines the library's manuscript copy of *Lovesongs of Connacht*; the text of *Ulysses* at this point includes a line of music. A. E. is ready to leave, and Eglinton asks if they will meet at Moore's that night for a poetry reading, to which both Buck Mulligan and Haines are invited. Stephen takes his exclusion from these plans as a snub. The literary discussion of *Hamlet* continues with Eglinton suggesting that Shakespeare most identified with Prince Hamlet. A worker enters, asking help from Mr. Lyster for a patron (Bloom) who wants to look at the newspaper called *Kilkenny People*. Stephen continues at length, mapping out supposed evidence in Shakespeare's plays of Hathaway's infidelity. At last, he and Mulligan leave the library, knocking past Bloom as they go out. Mulligan refers to Bloom as "the wandering jew" and also suggests that Bloom is a homosexual and is attracted sexually to Stephen.

WANDERING ROCKS

This long episode contains eighteen vignettes or small scenes that taken together give a sense of pedestrian traffic in Dublin between 3 p.m. and 4 p.m. It begins with the Catholic priest, Father John Conmee, who sets out about 3 p.m. to visit a school in the suburbs to see if Dignam's son can attend without charge. The episode concludes with the arrival of a cavalcade of the king's governor-general at the Mirus Park charity bazaar. These major treks weave through and around smaller scenes, some focusing on the principal characters, some on minor characters, and some on people who in a film would be called extras. Among these characters are a one-legged soldier; the dancing teacher, Mr. Maginni; Mrs. Breen, who earlier spoke with Bloom; and Corny Kelleher, the undertaker who handled the Dignam funeral. Two scenes occur at bookstalls. Stephen Dedalus pauses at a bookcart in Bedford

Row and is approached by his sister Dilly who asks him if the used French primer she has bought for a penny is any good. Elsewhere, Leopold Bloom selects the novel *Sweets of Sin* for Molly. At the Dedalus home, Stephen's sister Maggey boils shirts and his other sisters, Katey and Boody, lament the family's poverty. When Maggey says Dilly is out trying to find Simon, Boody responds, "Our father who art not in heaven." Martin Cunningham, who is involved in collecting money for Dignam's son, speaks to the subsheriff about the boy. Molly's arm appears at the second-floor window of the Bloom residence as she tosses a coin to the one-legged soldier who "crutche[s] himself" up Eccles Street. Blazes Boylan steps into a fruit shop and orders a basket to be sent ahead and looks down the open neckline of the shop girl's blouse as he asks to use the telephone. Across town, Boylan's secretary answers the phone and mentions his 4 p.m. appointment with Mr. Lenehan at the Ormond Hotel. Dilly waits in the street for her father and gets a shilling and two pennies from him. Through these and other tiny views of the street traffic, of people on footpaths, crossing bridges, and spitting out of open doors, the governor-general's carriage is spotted or missed as it makes its way out of town.

SIRENS

Two of the sirens in this episode, Ormond Hotel barmaids Lydia Douce and Mina Kennedy, lean out an upstairs window watching the cavalcade go by. The hotel is a meeting place for several groups of characters. Simon Dedalus enters the bar with Lenehan, looking for Boylan who arrives shortly. Elsewhere, Bloom buys stationery so that he can respond to Martha Clifford's letter and then goes into the Ormond with Richie Goulding to have some dinner and spy on Boylan. As Goulding and Bloom order drinks, Boylan leaves with Lenehan, causing Bloom to sob. In the bar, Simon Dedalus, Ben Dollard, and Bob Cowley recall concerts and discuss Molly Bloom's voice. The three sing together for the bar crowd, causing Bloom to think about how he once loaned Dollard evening clothes for a performance. Simon sings "M'appari," from an opera called *Martha*. Bloom listens, thinking about Dignam's funeral, about how music is mathematical, and about how his daughter Milly is not interested in music. The blind piano tuner taps his return to the hotel to pick up his tuning fork. As Boylan drives to Eccles Street and knocks at the Blooms' front door, Bloom hunches over the table, writing secretly to Martha. As he leaves the hotel, Bloom spots Bridie Kelly, a prostitute whose services he has used, and he turns away toward a shop window to avoid being recognized by her. He pretends to study a portrait displayed there of Robert Emmet and to read his last words. As a tram passes, he farts.

CYCLOPS

The Cyclops episode begins at 5 p.m. with a description of a near accident in which a chimney-sweep handles his brush carelessly and almost pokes out the eye of another person who is this episode's unnamed first-person narrator. This speaker, quite distinct in his use of language from the omniscient narrator whose voice appears repeatedly in other episodes, turns to give the sweep "the weight of [his] tongue." Indeed, the weightiness of the language in this episode is due to its pervasive vicious sarcasm and hyperbole. The narrator spies Joe Hynes and the two of them go off to Barney Kiernan's pub where they are joined by the unnamed citizen, who takes the lead in a loud, combative talk about politics, the Gold Cup horserace (which the twenty-to-one long shot Throwaway wins), and other matters, all of which culminates with a verbal attack on Leopold Bloom. The pub is across the street from the courthouse where Bloom has agreed to meet with Martin Cunningham and together travel out to Sandymount to visit Dignam's widow. As Bloom waits for Cunningham to arrive, the circle of drinkers in the pub enlarges, with O'Molloy, Lambert, Nolan, and Lenehan arriving after Bloom. The citizen's narrow-minded nationalistic and racist rant is counterpoised by Bloom's reasonableness and moderation. Bloom, the one non-drinker in the crowd and thus perceived by others to be giving offense on that count, remains broadminded, able to see more sides to the topics being discussed. In this way he inadvertently arouses the further ire of the citizen who, as Bloom spots Cunningham and leaves, runs into the street, yelling anti-Semitic remarks. Bloom and Cunningham escape into a carriage and pull away. This bombastic, ridiculous episode is complicated by thirty-two dispersed passages of extraordinarily inflated prose that present various styles and describe unrealistically other places and times, such as a courtroom scene, a public hanging, and action being taken in Parliament.

NAUSICAA

A third-person narrator in this episode uses language that parodies a second-rate sentimental novel, beginning with the description of Sandymount Strand and how "the summer evening had begun to fold the world in its mysterious embrace" and Gerty MacDowell, "as fair a specimen of winsome Irish girlhood as one could wish to see" with her "rosebud mouth." Gerty sits apart from her friends, Cissy Caffrey and Edy Boardman, who are playing on the beach and watching younger siblings, Cissy's little twin brothers and Edy's younger brother. Having visited Dignam's widow, Bloom has come to the beach. It is sometime between 4 p.m. and 5 p.m.; his watch stopped at 4:30. In a nearby church, evening mass is being celebrated with prayers to the Virgin Mary. Bloom watches Gerty, and she realizes it, positioning herself so he can look up her dress, exposing her thighs and underpants. With his hand in his pocket, Bloom masturbates, achieving orgasm as fireworks from the Mirus bazaar explode and viewers of the show sigh audibly. Bloom suspects his watch stopped at the very moment when Boylan and Molly engaged in sexual intercourse. Gerty gets up and walks away, revealing her limp.

OXEN OF THE SUN

Said by many, including Joyce himself, to be the most difficult episode in the novel, this inscrutable section presents the evolution of the English language through the parodied idiom of major texts and writers, all of which is divided into nine sections to match the months of gestation. It is 10 p.m. and various medical students drink and discuss rather boisterously a variety of topics related to sexuality and gestation in last delivered of her ninth son. Leopold Bloom is in the room with drunken Stephen Dedalus and others, called "right witty scholars," and while he hears their misogynistic and sacrilegious banter, he does not participate in it. Rather, as Mrs. Purefoy's baby is born, Bloom thinks sadly of Molly and the birth of their son, Rudy, who only lived a few days. Buck Mulligan arrives and takes center stage from Stephen. The nurse tries to quiet the young men, and eventually they decide to leave for a pub. Among the group is Alex Bannon, who speaks about his girlfriend and only gradually realizes she is Bloom's daughter, Milly. Bloom trails along, watching Stephen.

CIRCE

This episode, the longest of the novel at about one hundred and seventy pages, is presented in play format, with stage directions and speakers' names over their lines. It takes place about midnight in Nighttown, Dublin's red-light district, where the drunken Stephen and his buddies go, and Leopold Bloom follows along. The scenes of this play or drama are a series of hallucinations or fantasies, some of which must be induced by fatigue or alcohol. Separated from the young men, Bloom goes into an alley where he feeds a dog some meat he has purchased. This act engenders an hallucination in which Bloom is questioned and charged by two policemen. Witnesses, including the ghost of Dignam, seem to materialize to accuse him. Bloom heads into Bella Cohen's brothel, seeking Stephen. Inside, Stephen and Lynch are with two prostitutes, Florry and Kitty. Another fantasy or hallucination occurs in which Bloom is tyrannized by Bella Cohen, who accuses him of being less than a real man, a person who deserves to have the virile Boylan cuckolding him. Another prostitute, Zoe Higgins, accuses Bloom of being dominated by Molly. Stephen has an hallucination in which the ghost of his mother rises up and accuses him. This vision terrifies him, and he breaks away and runs outside, Bloom coming out after him. Outside there is a ruckus, and Stephen is knocked unconscious. Police come, but Corny Kelleher is nearby and helps resolve the tension. Abandoned by his friends, Stephen lies on the street, and Bloom looks over him, imagining he sees Rudy.

III: Nostos

EUMAEUS

After midnight, Bloom picks Stephen Dedalus up off the street and brushes him off. In this anticlimactic meeting between Bloom and Stephen, described in second-rate prose, the two walk arm-in-arm toward a cabman's shelter, a late-night place where winos and stray loners can find a cup of coffee. In the role of Good Samaritan, as an ordinary older man offering a young man regular kinds of advice, Bloom cautions the not-yet-sober Stephen about drinking too much and about going into Nighttown to the "women of ill fame" without knowing "a little juijitsu."

Along the way, they come across an acquaintance of Stephen, called Corley, who asks for money. Stephen gives him a halfcrown, much to Bloom's disapproval. Stephen remarks he has no place to sleep this night, and Bloom suggests Stephen go to his father's house. The two enter the cabman's shelter, which is operated by a man believed to be Skin-the-Goat Fitzharris, a person involved in the Phoenix Park murders. Here, Stephen and Bloom engage in conversation with a sailor who says his name is D. B. Murphy. When they exchange names, Murphy asks Stephen if he is related to Simon Dedalus. Stephen does not admit kinship, and Bloom offers that it must be a coincidence of names. Bloom looks at a paper and sees an article on the Gold Cup and one on Dignam's funeral, in which among the attendants listed are a "*M'Intosh*" and a person named "*L. Boom*." Talk turns to Parnell, and Bloom sympathizes more with Parnell and the married Kitty O'Shea than with O'Shea's husband, who Bloom assumes deserved his wife's betrayal. As chairs are inverted on tables, Bloom rises and takes Stephen outside, suggesting that the night air and a walk to Bloom's residence in Eccles Street will do the young man some good. Bloom offers a cup of cocoa at his house, and Stephen accepts. Street cleaners watch the two men go off, arm-in-arm.

ITHACA

This episode is narrated in a question-and-answer format, as might be seen in the dialogues of Socrates. According to Frank Delaney, in *James Joyce's "Odyssey,"* Joyce described this as "the form of a mathematical Catechism." It is 1 a.m. on Eccles Street at Leopold Bloom's residence, and Bloom discovers he does not have the key. He has to drop to the basement level and climb in through a window. Holding a candle, he opens the front door, and Stephen enters. They make their way to the back kitchen where they drink cups of cocoa. Bloom thinks maybe Stephen would be interested in Milly and invites him to stay the night, but Stephen declines. They talk about the Irish and Hebrew languages. About 1:30 a.m., they go out in the back, urinate side-by-side while observing a shooting star, and then separate. In his house again, Bloom sits in the front room, thinking about how he has spent his money on this day, about how his Dublin acquaintances are in bed and Dignam in his grave, about how he wishes he had enough money to buy a little house on the outskirts of town. He has observed evidence in the kitchen, front room, and elsewhere of Boylan's visit, and he thinks of Boylan as one of many suitors for Molly, one in a series. The music for "Love's Old Sweet Song," is open on the piano. At 2 a.m., he goes upstairs to bed, lying down with his feet next to Molly's head and his head at her feet. He kisses her buttocks, and she awakes slightly. He tells her about his day, lying about some details. It has been over ten years since they engaged in sexual intercourse. This episode ends with a big dot, like an oversized period, marking the spot, the conclusion.

PENELOPE

According to Frank Delaney, Joyce described this episode as "amplitudinously curvilinear." Delaney further explains that the first sentence contains twenty-five hundred words, that there are eight sentences in all, and the episode begins and ends, again quoting Joyce, with "the most positive word in the English language, the word *yes*." Commonly referred to as Molly Bloom's soliloquy, this episode presents in stream-of-consciousness style her drowsy reverie.

Her first sentence begins with her surprise at Bloom's request that she serve him breakfast in bed the next morning, ordering up two eggs before he falls asleep. She wonders if Bloom has reached orgasm during the day. She compares Boylan's aggressive sexual style to Bloom's and then thinks about the Breens' marriage, concluding that hers and Leopold's is better. In the next sentence, Molly thinks about men who have admired her, listing several of them. She wonders if she will get together with Boylan again and thinks of their upcoming concert trip to Belfast. Among her many thoughts, she considers losing some weight and wishes Bloom had a better paying office job. In the third sentence, she thinks about how attractive breasts are and how unattractive male genitals are.

She thinks about how Bloom admires her breasts and once suggested she express milk from them into their tea. Molly thinks back to her early years in Gibraltar, and her friend Hester Stanhope. She recalls how lonely she felt after Hester and her husband moved away. She also thinks about Milly and how she got a card from their daughter while Leopold received a letter.

The fifth sentence includes memory of her first love interest, Lieutenant Mulvey, whom she knew in Gibraltar. A train whistles in the distance, making her think of "Love's Old Sweet Song," which she has been practicing for an upcoming concert. In the next sentence, Molly thinks of her daughter, who is studying photography in Mullingar. She thinks about how pretty Milly is, quite like Molly herself was in her teens. Molly senses she is beginning to menstruate and gets up to use the chamber pot. In the seventh sentence, back in bed, Molly muses about Leopold's finances, how she and he have moved several times. She wonders if he spent money this day on other women and wonders how much he offered at Dignam's funeral. She thinks of Bloom's circle of male acquaintances and about Simon Dedalus's good singing voice. She recalls meeting Stephen when he was a little boy. In the eighth sentence, she ponders the fact that Leopold does not hug her any more. She thinks of Stephen's mother recently dead and of Rudy's death. She thinks about morning and about the possibility of telling Leopold about her sexual encounter with Boylan, her first extramarital involvement. She thinks she will buy flowers for the house, in case

Stephen returns. Finally, she thinks of being with Leopold sixteen years earlier at Howth, how he called her "a flower of the mountain" and proposed to her, and how she accepted him:

> I put my arms around him yes and
> drew him down to me so he could
> feel my breasts all perfume yes and
> his heart was going like mad and yes
> I said yes I will Yes.

Following these memorable lines, the places and dates for the composition of the novel are given: "*Trieste-Zürich-Paris, 1914-1921*.

Characters

A. E.

The pseudonym of George Russell, A. E. is a highly respected Irish poet. He associates with other established literary people, a group which includes Haines and Mulligan but which excludes Stephen Dedalus, though he wishes to be a member.

Richard Best

Richard Best, a librarian at the National Library, takes part in the Scylla and Charybdis episode discussion of *Hamlet*. His comments represent conventional views of the play.

Leopold Bloom

Leopold Bloom, a thirty-eight-year-old canvasser, lives with his wife Marion at 7 Eccles Street in Dublin. Bloom is an empathetic, sensitive, earthy, sensual person who responds to the weather, to the smell of organ meat cooking, to women he sees on the street, and who puzzles over laws of physical science. He loves his daughter, fifteen-year-old Milly, and still mourns for his son Rudy, who died when he was a baby about eleven years earlier. On June 16, 1904, Bloom attends a funeral, visits a newspaper office and the National Library, has dinner at a hotel, and meets up with Stephen Dedalus in a brothel and invites him home. On this day in Dublin, Leopold Bloom anticipates and dreads his wife's infidelity with Blazes Boylan, yet he himself continues a clandestine correspondence with Martha Clifford and masturbates on Sandymount beach as he watches Gerty MacDowell.

Marion Bloom

Voluptuous Marion Bloom, called Molly, is thirty-four years old and a professional singer. Her father was a British officer, and her mother, Lunita Laredo, was a Spanish Jew. Molly grew up in Gibraltar, and presumably she moved to Dublin with her father sometime in 1886. Since the neonatal death of her second child, Rudy, she has not had a sexual relationship with her husband or any other man, but on this day, while he is away from home, she has a sexual encounter with Hugh Boylan.

Millicent Bloom

Millicent Bloom, called Milly, is the fifteen-year-old daughter of Leopold and Molly Bloom. She lives in Mullingar and is studying to become a photographer. On this day, Leopold enjoys a letter from Milly, in which she thanks him and her mother for birthday gifts.

Hugh Boylan

Hugh Boylan, called Blazes, is Molly Bloom's concert manager. Boylan is a womanizer, a fancy dresser, and man about town. He walks in slick, highly polished shoes and his car jingles through the streets making a sound reminiscent of Molly's bedsprings.

Josie Powell Breen

Josie Breen was years earlier a girlfriend of Leopold Bloom. She is now the wife of Dennis Breen, a paranoid who requires a lot of her attention and care.

The Citizen

This unnamed character, prominent in the "Cyclops" episode, is a vitriolic, narrow-minded nationalist, in favor of a free Ireland and willing to blame social ills on foreigners, especially Jews. In the pub, he verbally attacks Leopold Bloom, who responds logically and withdraws quickly. The citizen is the kind of man who sits around in a pub waiting for someone else to buy him a few drinks and then sounds off in a political harangue.

Martha Clifford

Martha Clifford writes letters to Leopold Bloom, whom she does not know face-to-face, addressing him by his pseudonym, Henry Flower.

Martha's letters indicate that she is poorly educated and not particularly daring in pursuing a sexual relationship with Bloom. Yet she enjoys the titillation of their clandestine correspondence.

Bella Cohen

Bella Cohen is the madam in charge of the brothel that Stephen Dedalus and his friends visit in Nighttown. She is domineering, with a large build. Concerned with appearances, she attacks the rowdy visitors in her establishment.

Martin Cunningham

One of the mourners at Patrick Dignam's funeral, Martin Cunningham takes the initiative to start a collection for Dignam's widow and son. He is sympathetic and kindly, speaking up on Bloom's behalf several times during the day. In the late afternoon, he and Bloom visit Dignam's widow in Sandymount Strand.

Garrett Deasy

Misogynistic, anti-Semitic Garrett Deasy is the headmaster of the boys' school where Stephen teaches history. Mr. Deasy has written an essay on hoof-and-mouth disease and wants it published in local papers. He gives it to Stephen, asking him to present it to the newspaper editors with whom he is acquainted. He suspects that Stephen is not suited to a professional life in teaching.

Dilly Dedalus

Dilly Dedalus, one of Simon's daughters and Stephen's sister, has as much natural intelligence as Stephen has, but she is unlikely to have his opportunities to become learned. Nonetheless, she seeks to become educated and with a penny buys a used French primer in order to study the language. She waits on the street to get a shilling from her father and take the money home to her sisters who are washing shirts there and would have virtually nothing to eat were it not for the soup brought to them by a local nun.

Simon Dedalus

Father of Stephen and four daughters, Simon Dedalus recently buried his wife May and still mourns her. Simon has quite a good singing voice and likes to entertain his drinking friends with funny stories. Born in Cork and once rather successful, Simon has recently had financial problems. During this day, he spends money in pubs, doing nothing to help or protect his daughters at home. Simon is highly critical of Stephen, and when Stephen is asked if Simon is his father, Stephen demurs.

Stephen Dedalus

Recently home in Dublin from a year or two in Paris where he studied medicine, Stephen Dedalus is an intellectual and would-be poet, a well-read young man who takes himself very seriously and is depressed after his mother's recent death and his ongoing alienation from Ireland and the Catholic Church. A teacher at a boys' school, Stephen spends his time talking about his literary theories and drinking with his friends. At this point in his life, he is aware of having not found his professional place. He dissociates himself from his sisters and is alienated from his father, Simon.

Ben Dollard

A drinking friend of Simon Dedalus, Ben Dollard has a good voice and enjoys singing in pubs. He performs with Simon at the Ormond Hotel.

Lydia Douce

Lydia Douce is a barmaid at the Ormond Hotel. She has a crush on Boylan. She and Mina Kennedy are seen hanging out the second-floor window watching the viceregal cavalcade go by in the streets below.

John Eglinton

A published essayist, John Eglinton spends time in the National Library, where he hears Stephen expound on his theory about *Hamlet*. He finds Stephen over-confident and egotistical.

Richard Goulding

Suffering from chronic back pain, Richard Goulding, called Richie, has dinner with Bloom at the Ormond Hotel. Goulding is the brother of the deceased May Dedalus and thus Stephen's uncle.

Haines

An Englishman who is temporarily staying at the Martello Tower with Buck Mulligan and Stephen Dedalus, Haines has a bad dream during the night of June 15, waking the others by shooting a gun at an imagined tiger. Later, on June 16, Haines, an Oxford student, socializes with Buck and other literati, who exclude Stephen from their circle.

Joe Hynes

A local newspaper reporter, Joe Hynes borrows three pounds from Leopold Bloom but conveniently forgets to pay back the loan. He meets the narrator of the Cyclops episode in the street and accompanies him to Barney Kiernan's pub for a conversation with an unnamed character referred to as the citizen.

Corny Kelleher

Corny Kelleher is the undertaker who officiates at Patrick Dignam's funeral and is later seen in his shop doorway. Corny intervenes on their behalf when Stephen Dedalus and Leopold Bloom get involved with two policemen on the street near Nighttown.

Mina Kennedy

Mina Kennedy is a barmaid at the Ormond Hotel. She and Lydia Douce flirt with their male customers. Blond Mina is more reserved than Lydia. Both women are seen hanging out the second-floor window watching the viceregal cavalcade go by in the streets below.

Lenehan

Lenehan is a sports editor for a local Dublin newspaper. Disliked by Molly Bloom, Lenehan makes fun of Leopold Bloom. He is a friend of Simon Dedalus.

Lynch

An old friend of Stephen Dedalus, Lynch is a medical student. He is involved with the prostitute, Kitty Ricketts.

Thomas W. Lyster

Quaker librarian at the National Library, Thomas Lyster patiently hears Stephen expound on his *Hamlet* theory and is open-minded about it.

Gerty MacDowell

Gerty MacDowell is influenced by romance literature and women's magazines and takes special care of her clothes and skin. She dreams of meeting a strong, handsome man who will marry her. Bloom is sexually aroused by her when he sees her on Sandymount Strand in the Nausicaa episode.

John Henry Menton

John Menton was once Leopold Bloom's rival for Molly. A lawyer by trade, Menton was Patrick Dignam's boss. Menton looks down on Bloom.

Malachi Mulligan

Popular Malachi Mulligan, called Buck, is a medical student and friend of Stephen Dedalus. Buck is lively, theatrical, and able to satirize anything. He is well-read and tells funny, off-color jokes. Neither Bloom nor Simon Dedalus thinks well of Buck.

J. J. O'Molloy

J. J. O'Molloy is an unemployed lawyer who on this day is unable to borrow money. At Barney Kiernan's pub, he defends Bloom.

Topics for Further Study

- Spend several hours walking around your neighborhood, noting people you see and events as they occur. Later, make a map of your journey and write a story about it.

- Read *Portrait of the Artist as a Young Man* and then write a paper about what you learn in this novel about Stephen Dedalus that helps clarify the portrait of him in *Ulysses*.

- Research patterns of alcohol consumption and alcoholism in Dublin, Ireland. Using whatever statistics you can find, make a graph that shows changing levels of alcohol consumption in three different decades of the twentieth century.

- Read Frank McCourt's novel *Angela's Ashes* and write a paper on how alcoholism affected McCourt's family.

- Do some research on the literary technique of stream of consciousness. Then study a couple of pages of Molly Bloom's monologue and trace the sequence of her thoughts. Write a paper that shows how the sequence of thoughts reveals her personality.

Kitty Ricketts

A prostitute with aspirations for a better life, Kitty Ricketts dates Lynch.

George Russell

See A. E.

Florry Talbot

One of the prostitutes at Bella Cohen's establishment, Florry Talbot entertains the medical students who visit the brothel with Stephen.

The Modern Hero

Ulysses has as its hero a most ordinary man, Leopold Bloom. So unlike the muscular, militaristic Homeric hero whose name serves as the novel's title, Bloom is gentle, self-effacing, reserved, and peripheralized. Arguably more associated with home than the outer world, even though on this day he spends most of his time out about town, the kindly, other-centered Bloom is first depicted making breakfast for his wife and feeding the cat. He is a caring man, deeply attached to his wife and daughter and continuing to mourn the neonatal death of his son, Rudy. Whereas Ulysses welcomes adventures in strange and threatening places and has a crew of sailors he orders about, Bloom lives an ordinary man's life and is a loner, an outsider, a Jew, a man who thinks about the physical world but chooses not to interfere, a man who lives very much in his body, responsive to women, courteous toward men, sensual in an unobtrusive way. He admires women on the street, wonders sympathetically about a woman in protracted labor, and talks politely to a childhood sweetheart. He helps a blind man cross the street, he tells an acquaintance his hat has a ding in it, and he kindly reminds someone of a loan and does not take offense when the man seems to brush him off.

While the daring epic hero slays the Cyclops and navigates between the rocks of Scylla and the whirlpool of Charybdis, Bloom maneuvers among offensive others, seeking to engage with them peacefully, deferring to others and not taking offense even when he is directly insulted. He dresses in black out of respect for a friend's funeral and gives generously to the collection taken up for the man's widow. While the epic hero is defined by his conquests, his ego, his self-centeredness, Bloom is defined by his small gestures of kindness, his thoughtfulness of others and of the physical world, and his polite social restraint.

Sad about his wife's infidelity, he is resigned rather than defensive or controlling. Though their marriage is sexless, he is not without desire. He becomes aroused while looking at Gerty MacDowell on the beach, but he satisfies his desire privately, without imposing it on her, and his thoughts here and elsewhere inevitably return to Molly, so comfortably is he bound to her. In many ways, Leopold Bloom is the antithesis of the classical Ulysses; he is not a world traveler or an adventurer; he is not larger-than-life, and he is not able to perform extraordinary feats. In this character, Joyce affirms what is extraordinary about an ordinary man's character; he provides a new sense of the heroic, written in the small-scale actions of a twentieth-century urban man, in his kindliness in the face of alienation, in his ability to calmly analyze differences, in his civic decency.

The Artist's Search for a Place in the World

Stephen Dedalus is a would-be poet, a well-schooled young man full of academic theories and familiar texts. In a sense homeless (he rents a place that is usurped by others, he is back in Ireland only temporarily, he has nowhere to sleep in this day), Stephen expresses the discomfort and ennui of a creative spirit who has not yet found his medium or made his mark. Like the young Icarus, the son of the mythological Dedalus, Stephen has yet to test his wings, and perhaps like the mythic son, he may fail when he does. He is hampered, he says, by two masters, the government of England that controls Ireland and the Catholic Church that clutches his conscience. Without the role model of a suitable father, Stephen drifts in Dublin literary society, working at a job that bores him, excluded by literary insiders he wishes to displace. His plight in part results from his age: he is just starting out, and he is at this moment hampered by grief and guilt concerning his mother. On a larger scale, his plight is a product of feeling trapped by a social context which is itself fettered by poverty and alcoholism.

Stream of Consciousness

The stream-of-consciousness novel takes as its subject the interior thought sequence and patterns of associations which distinguish characters from one another. According to *A Handbook to Literature*, the stream-of-consciousness novel assumes that what matters most about human existence is how it is experienced subjectively. The interior level of experience is idiosyncratic, illogical, and disjointed and the "pattern of free psychological association … determines the shifting sequence of thought and feeling." The work of Sigmund Freud (1856-1939) offered a structure and way of understanding different psychological levels or areas of consciousness, and some modern writers, such as Joyce, Virginia Woolf, and William Faulkner, drew upon Freud's theories as they used the stream-of-consciousness style.

In the eighteenth and nineteenth centuries, many English novels focused more on outer rather than inner events, and the plot was usually arranged in a linear fashion (as it is, for example, in Charles Dickens's *David Copperfield*). Typically, when these novels traced the inner thoughts and feelings of characters, they did so within the single idiom of the narrator. In Joyce's handling, the spontaneous flow of thoughts and associations which typify one character is presented in that person's own idiom or voice. In part, what Joyce undertakes in *Ulysses* is to write the novel from the inner world of characters' interior thinking, using their idiosyncratic language patterns.

In his review of the novel, Edmund Wilson explains that whereas earlier novelists presented their characters' inner thoughts in "one vocabulary and cadence," Joyce communicates "the consciousness of each of the characters … made to speak in the idiom proper to it." In this way, as Wilson explains, "Joyce manages to give the effect of unedited human minds, drifting aimlessly along from one triviality to another." For the inexperienced reader who brings to the novel expectations based on the nineteenth-century novel, the challenge is huge. Such a reader assumes that the novel will present first things first, that its characters will be introduced, that relationships will be explicit and clear, and so forth. However, in the case of *Ulysses*, the reader must experience the world of the novel from within each subjective consciousness as it is presented.

Autobiographical Novel

Ulysses is, in part, the portrait of Joyce as a slightly older young artist, back from Paris at the time of his mother's death and staying for a while in the Martello Tower rented by his friend, Oliver St. John Gogart. Joyce was educated by Jesuits, and in 1904, he taught in a boys' school in Dalkey, about a mile from the Martello Tower. Among his literary friends, he pronounced all manner of theories, not least of which was his biographical interpretation of *Hamlet*, and, with a fine tenor voice, he pursued a singing career, entering a singing competition and giving a couple of performances in the summer of 1904. The portrait in *Ulysses* of the feckless Simon Dedalus is based on John Joyce, and the Dedalus sisters reside at the same address in the novel that the Joyce family resided in that year: 7 St. Peter's Terrace, Cabra. The choice of June 16, 1904, as the time for this novel honors Joyce's first date with Nora Barnacle, an illiterate hotel maid who became the author's long-time companion and years later his beloved wife. Although Joyce was no longer as young as Stephen Dedalus is portrayed in *Portrait of the Artist as a Young Man*, and Stephen in *Ulysses* has not yet proved himself as a writer and artist, Joyce nonetheless identified closely with Stephen Dedalus. Stephen's moodiness, his egocentrism, and his creative puns and extensive web of literary and religious allusions parallel Joyce's own manner of thinking and speaking and express the author's feelings about Ireland and Catholicism.

Allusion

There are thousands of literary allusions in *Ulysses*, the countless corollaries to Homer's epic being only one constellation of correspondences. One recurrent allusion is to Shakespeare's *Hamlet*. The play is mentioned in the first episode, with comparisons drawn between Stephen's moodiness and the depressed self-absorption of Prince Hamlet and between the Danish castle and the Martello Tower. The allusion to *Hamlet* is prominent also in the Scylla and Charybdis episode, which takes place at the National Library. Here, Stephen Dedalus expounds on his biographical reading of *Hamlet*, basing his theory on suppositional information about Shakespeare's life. The theory, which he admits not believing himself, argues that Shakespeare identified with King Hamlet's ghost, that Prince Hamlet is aligned with Shakespeare's son, Hamnet, who died as a child, and that Queen Gertrude is the equivalent of the unfaithful Ann Hathaway. Using this play as a referent and embedding this theory in the novel, Joyce capitalizes on certain themes well known to readers familiar with Shakespeare's play. Parallels are suggested between the deceased King Hamlet, the betrayed husband and father of Prince Hamlet, and Leopold Bloom, who has an unfaithful wife and serves somewhat as a surrogate father for Stephen. There are other allusions to *Hamlet*: Stephen is apparently ousted by the so-called usurper Buck Mulligan (just as Hamlet's ascension to the throne is thwarted by his uncle, Claudius); and the tentative step-father relationship Stephen forms with Bloom may be an inexact reference to Hamlet's uneasy relationship with Claudius. The literary allusion offers a point of departure or contrast by which the present text can be understood. This is a novel much about a son's longing for a father (Homer set it up that way to begin with), and *Hamlet* is a

Renaissance referent that also explores this theme. Joyce toys with the ideas of paternity and legacy and examines the forces that disrupt context and inheritance, situating his novel within the classical framework and extending it to Shakespeare's play, among probably hundreds of other well-known and lesser-known texts, all in order to place his novel in a literary tradition of which it is a product and which it aims to reroute. His assumption throughout is that the reader has read as much as he has.

Compare & Contrast

- **1900s:** The eighteenth-century Martello Tower in which James Joyce lives in 1904 is a rented apartment, one of many small defensive forts built along Dublin Bay to defend the island against possible attack by Napoleon.
  Today: The Martello Tower is the site of the James Joyce Museum, a tourist stop for people who want to walk in the footsteps of Stephen Dedalus and Leopold Bloom.

- **1900s:** Ireland is predominantly a one-religion country with 85 percent of its population devout Catholics.
  Today: Still predominantly Catholic, Ireland is increasingly secular, and prohibitions by the Catholic Church on reproduction

matters are ignored by increasing numbers of Irish people.

- **1900s:** While estimates on Irish consumption of alcohol are unavailable, the pub serves as a daily meeting place where the Irish drink, discuss local matters and politics, and sing along with musicians who gather together informally.

  Today: Between 1992 and 2002, estimates place the consumption rate of alcohol among the Irish as among the highest in Europe at 14.2 liters per adult annually.

Irish Struggle for Independence: From the 1860s to World War I

The term, home rule, refers to an Irish movement for legislative independence for Ireland from the United Kingdom, which began in the 1860s. In 1874, advocates for home rule won fifty-six seats in the House of Commons, and these men formed an Irish party of sorts in Westminster, led by Isaac Butts. Butts was followed by William Shaw in 1879 and by Charles Stewart Parnell in 1880. As Parnell led the movement, advocates for home rule won eighty-six seats in the 1885 parliamentary election and supported the liberal government of Prime Minister William Ewart Gladstone, who introduced the first home rule bill. It was defeated in 1886 in the House of Commons. Gladstone introduced a second bill in 1892, which passed through the House of Commons but was defeated in the House of Lords. The third time such a bill was presented to the House of Commons occurred in 1912 by Prime Minister Herbert Henry Asquith. This third piece of legislation passed the House of Commons, but in the House of Lords, a veto move was used to stall discussion for two years, by which time World War I had begun and Parliament decided to postpone discussion of home rule until after the conclusion of the war.

The Rise and Fall of Parnell

Charles Stewart Parnell is buried in Glasnevin, where in the novel May Dedalus is buried and Patrick Dignam's body is laid to rest. In the Lestrygonians episode, Parnells brother, John Howard Parnell, is spotted in the corner of a pub, and in the Cyclops and Eumaeus episodes, Parnell is heatedly discussed, Bloom siding privately with Parnell rather than contributing to criticism of him. Indeed, by 1904, Parnell was, in every sense, gone but not forgotten.

Born June 27, 1846, Charles Stewart Parnell was educated at the University of Cambridge and became politically active as a young man when he began supporting the work of Isaac Butts for home rule. Parnell was elected to the House of Commons in 1874, and once there, he pursued an obstructionist policy, using filibusters to stall legislation and bring political and public attention to conditions and sentiments in Ireland. In 1879, Parnell headed the recently formed National Land League, which sought ultimately to remove English landlords from Ireland. When Parnell urged a boycott, he was arrested, and from Kilmainham Prison he issued a manifesto, inciting Irish peasants to refuse to pay their rent to English landlords. After this, he and Prime Minister Gladstone reached what was called the Kilmainham Treaty, in which the no-rent policy was abandoned and Parnell urged Irish people to avoid violence. Parnell was released on May 2, 1882, and just four days later, the chief secretary and undersecretary for Ireland, Lord

Frederick Charles Cavendish and Thomas Burke, were murdered in Phoenix Park, Dublin, an event alluded to in the cabstand discussion in the Eumaeus episode and elsewhere in *Ulysses*. Much speculation surrounded the identity of the assassins, since this crime so effectively sabotaged Parnell's new strategy for peace in partnership with Gladstone's resolve to work for reform. Ultimately, the radical militant group, the Irish Invincibles, took responsibility for or was assigned responsibility for the murders. The aftermath was a split between Parnell and Gladstone, culminating in the end of the prime minister's government.

The death knell of Parnell's effectiveness as a leader sounded with the 1889 divorce case brought by Lieutenant William Henry O'Shea, a loyal supporter of Parnell, who named Parnell in an adultery charge. Proven guilty of this extramarital alliance in 1890, Parnell was ruined. He and Katherine O'Shea, who had been lovers for years, were married shortly after the O'Shea divorce was granted, causing further public scandal among both Irish and English, which exacerbated the divisions among the nationalists. Parnell fought in vain for the reunification of the nationalists until his death at Brighton on October 6, 1891. The schism persisted and contributed to the further delay of the discussion of home rule when World War I erupted.

Critical Overview

Highlighting both the strengths and limitations of the novel, Edmund Wilson's 1922 review in *New Republic* is an excellent starting place for evaluating the critical reviews garnered by *Ulysses*. Wilson applauds the work for its "high genius," and at the same time, he asserts that Joyce "has written some of the most unreadable chapters in the whole history of fiction." Wilson calls Joyce's "technical triumph … the most faithful X-ray ever taken of the ordinary human consciousness." Wilson explains that Joyce shows all the ignobility of common people in such a way that readers sympathize with and respect them. According to Wilson, Joyce demonstrates "his extraordinary poetic faculty for investing particular incidents with universal significance." Yet Wilson faults Joyce's work on two counts: first, its form is dictated by the form of the *Odyssey* rather than emerging from its own immediate content; second, his literary imitative parody "interposes a heavy curtain between" readers and the novel's characters.

Frank Delaney described the divide among other critics in the 1920s:

> When the novel appeared … there seemed to be only two schools of thought—and criticism. Ford Madox Ford wrote: 'One feels admiration that is almost reverence for the incredible labours of this incredible

genius.' But Alfred Noyes suggested that it was 'the foulest book that has ever found its way into print.'

Delaney quotes W. B. Yeats who commented that *Ulysses* amounted to "the vulgarity of a single Dublin day prolonged to seven hundred pages." Delaney also notes that the *Sunday Express* held that *Ulysses* was "The most infamously obscene book in ancient or modern literature"; and the *Daily Express* agreed: "Our first impression is that of sheer disgust."

It was the Nausicaa episode which brought about the U.S. charge of obscenity and caused the *Little Review* to stop publishing installments of the novel. This decision led to the publication of the novel in France. After that, the furor brought attention to the novel and to Joyce, who was exonerated by the U.S. district court decision that the novel was not prurient. Joyce himself made little money from the novel, but when it "emerged from copyright" in 1992, many presses hurried to print and profit from the novel, as an anonymous reviewer explains in the January 18, 1992, *Economist*. Cyril Connolly in a 1999 issue of *New Statesman* mildly reports on the "revolutionary" technique that made it possible for Joyce "to create a mythical universe of his own." But he points out that Joyce was so much a part of the novel his "clock seemed literally to have stopped on June 16th, 1904."

The degree to which this revolutionary and controversial work came to be accepted is indicated in the widespread celebration of the one hundredth anniversary of what is called Bloomsday, on June 16, 2004. The occasion brought forth festivities, readings, and renewed critical attention for the novel. For example, two articles appeared in *Commonweal*. In one, Robert H. Bell writes of the "the enduring power" of *Ulysses*, which "has become the canonical twentieth-century novel." In the other, which is especially beautifully written, Mark Patrick Hederman describes the festival held in Dublin in 2004 and the new James Joyce Bridge that was opened on Bloomsday in 2004. He notes the irony that the country which initially "condemned and reviled" the work now makes Joyce "an Irish industry." Hederman points to the fact that *Ulysses* "describes the paralysis" of Dublin, depicting how "The twin forces of politics and religion had entrapped the Irish in alcoholism, sexual repression, and poverty." Writing of the improvements in the city and its culture since Joyce abandoned it in 1904, Hederman remarks that Joyce in a sense showed Dubliners the way to embrace "the new century's awareness of human possibility." He concludes that "Joyce's magisterial work … incorporates the whole of humanity, unconscious as well as conscious."

What Do I Read Next?

- To prepare for reading *Ulysses*, people should first read James Joyce's *Dubliners* and then his *Portrait of the Artist as a Young Man* (both available from Norton [2005]), because *Ulysses* in a sense is the sequel to the collection of stories and the autobiographical novel.

- Originally published in 1930 and reprinted several times by Vintage Books, Stuart Gilbert's *James Joyce's "Ulysses"* is the essential starting place for decoding the novel. Gilbert worked closely with Joyce and got the author's approval for this interpretation of the novel. Gilbert's writing is formal and complex, but it expresses the vision of the novel Joyce himself hoped to impart to readers.

- Richard Ellmann wrote *James Joyce*, the definitive biography of Joyce, published by Oxford University Press in 1983.

- Virginia Woolf's *Mrs. Dalloway* (1925) is a stream-of-consciousness novel about a day in the post-World War I London life of Clarissa Dalloway, wife of a member of Parliament, as she prepares to give a party that night. An excellent annotated edition edited by Mark Hussey appeared in 2005.

Sources

Bell, Robert H., "Bloomsday at 100," in *Commonweal*, Vol. 131, No. 10, May 21, 2004, pp. 15-17.

Connolly, Cyril, "Joyce Remembered," in *New Statesman*, Vol. 128, No. 4464, November 29, 1999, p. 55.

Delaney, Frank, *James Joyce's Odyssey: A Guide to the Dublin of "Ulysses,"* Holt, Rinehart, and Winston, 1981, pp. 9, 10, 18, 21, 89, 166, 176.

Ellmann, Richard, *Ulysses on the Liffey*, Oxford University Press, 1972, pp. xi, xiii, xvii.

Gifford, Don, and Robert J. Seidman, *"Ulysses" Annotated: Notes for James Joyce's "Ulysses,"* University of California Press, 1988, p. 16.

Hederman, Mark Patrick, "{Bloomsday at 100} in *Commonweal*, Vol. 131, No. 10, May 21, 2004, pp. 17-18.

Holman, C. Hugh, and William Harmon, *A Handbook to Literature*, Macmillan, 1986, p. 484.

Joyce, James, *Ulysses*, Vintage Books, 1990.

"Pull Out His Eyes, Apologize: James Joyce and His Interpreters," in *Economist*, Vol. 322, No. 7742, January 18, 1992, p. 91.

Schwarz, Daniel R., "Joyce's Schema for *Ulysses*," in *Reading Joyce's "Ulysses,"* St. Martin's Press,

1987, pp. 277-80.

Wilson, Edmund, Review of *Ulysses*, in *New Republic*, July 5, 1922, http://www.tnr.com/doc.mhtml? i=classic&s=Wilson070522 (accessed July 27, 2006).

Further Reading

Bulson, Eric, *James Joyce: An Introduction*, Cambridge University Press, 2006.

> This introduction presents the essential information that will make reading Joyce's works easier for the beginner.

Emig, Rainer, ed., *"Ulysses": James Joyce*, Palgrave Macmillan, 2005.

> This collection of recent essays gives an overview of scholarship on Joyce's novel and the divergent readings the novel has generated. Among the theoretical approaches included are gender and deconstruction.

Homer, *Odyssey*, translated by Robert Fagles, Penguin Group, 2006.

> Homer's classical epic of the mythic journey home by Odysseus is translated by Fagles into modern idiom, making this the edition to choose for a first read.

Kertész, Imre, *Kaddish for a Child Not Born*, translated by Christopher C. Wilson and Katharina M. Wilson, Northwestern University Press, 1997.

> This whole novel is a single,

unbroken interior monologue in which the protagonist, a Holocaust survivor, reflects on his past, his childhood, a failed marriage, and his decision not to have children.

Milton Keynes UK
Ingram Content Group UK Ltd.
UKHW021309230823
427358UK00025B/549